OWN your OWN Happiness

Life Journal with Anetita

By: Annette Avila

This journal belongs to:

_____

Own your own Happiness Copyright © 2023 Annette Avila
No portion of this book may be reproduced in any form without written permission from the publisher or author, except as permitted by U.S. copyright law.

ISBN: 9798874416720

Made in the USA

Table of Contents

Prologue	5
Part one	15
Gratitude	18
Exercise 1	19
Awareness	21
Exercise 2	23
Discovery	33
Exercise 3	34
Happiness	41
Exercise 4	44
Attention	57
Exercise 5	59
Stress	66
Exercise 6	70
Think: Stress=Positive	76
Exercise 7	77

Today is the first day of the rest of your life. My dad is the one to say this frequently. Okay Dad. We get it! It took me forty years to understand what he was talking about. Forty years to finally feel peace within me. I've never been more grateful than now. I appreciate everything around me and don't take anything for granted.

Prologue

Wife, mother, daughter, educator and happiness life coach. I was born on December 11, 1982 in Laredo, Texas. I grew up with both my parents and my siblings. My parents were both coming from divorces and when they married, we had a family of eight. My father was a teacher. My mother had her own school for about 17 years. I remember that by age eight or nine I would go with my mother to her school and help during the summer months. I'd go from classroom to classroom helping the gymnastics teacher, swimming instructor, chef, taking care of the kids and assisting in any way. When my father would take us to his high school where he'd teach, I'd help him grade papers. I was very fortunate to have found my purpose in life at such an early age and I have my parents to thank for that.

By age 16 I started working at my aunt's daycare. I was my own little teacher taking care of 4-6 year olds. They used to assign the rooms by colors. I was in charge of the green room. My parents bought me so many scrubs for the week. I'd go to school in the morning and because I had more credits, I would get out early in the afternoon and take off straight to work. Two years later I graduated from high school in 2001 and went straight to receive my associates degree in Interdisciplinary studies.

    I received my Bachelors in August 2007 and had my first interview in October of that same year. I walked into the principal's office for the interview (back then it was just one person, unlike now. You enter a conference room and you have an administrator and teachers from different grade levels or committees; now that's nerve wrecking!)I was carrying a big tote bag with multiple copies of my resumes and school supplies(I don't know what I was thinking, or if I was just overpacking for a trip). We spoke for about 30 minutes or so and I remember her asking me, "So, when can you start?" I was ready and determined and said, "I can start today."

    I got called within 2 days and started on Monday, October 30, 2007. Years later my principal described me as Mary Poppins walking into a room holding a bag full of goodies.

    So now imagine me. My first of everything; job, car, apartment. I was in a "high moment" in my life and why not! I felt that I could do anything and be anything I wanted. My first paycheck went to getting hair laser removal. Which turned out to be a waste of money. I had paid everything upfront, went for about 3 sessions or so and in the following session the place no longer existed. I walked around the building and could see nothing but emptiness. Place had shut down and no way of tracing or contacting them. This little shenanigan cost about fifteen hundred dollars. The following month I went to purchase my own apartment. After that, my first owned vehicle. A white pontiac solstice. It was exhilarating like the drive to have control of my life. I was in a high moment and no one could take that away.

    I met my first husband (there's only two, calm down) there at school and we started dating the following year. We were expecting by the end of July and got married in November of 2008. One month before my due date, we had been arguing over something. I can't remember. I was driving south on the loop heading to work and was driving in the middle lane. Suddenly to my left, I see a car that starts moving towards my lane and my reaction was to jerk the wheel to the right hand side then back to the left. The car noticed me and also went back to his lane. The only thing that I could remember was my car spinning round and round. Simultaneously my car was also advancing forward. I remember that I was telling myself "calm down Annette, this is just like a carnival ride, you're okay, baby is going to be okay, just control yourself." Next thing I know, I was about 200 feet away and the paramedic had arrived and was asking me if I was part of the accident. What accident? I was the accident! I turned around to look at the traffic on the northbound side, opposite of the direction that I was heading, and witnessed the "accident" which was about a six car collision. It turns out that the car that jerked back to his lane had also lost control and had jumped over the median and caused cars to crash and pile up on each other. I was taken to the emergency room to make sure everything was fine. I had been able to keep my composure and hadn't even dilated.

On March, Friday the 13th of 2009, I remember getting contractions at school and drove myself to the hospital. My baby boy was born.

Later on that year in September, we were heading to the store to buy some fajitas and tortillas. I was sitting in the back with my little boy in his car seat (he was about 6 months old) when suddenly I couldn't see him on the right hand side. The first thing that crossed my mind was that someone had taken him in a blink of an eye. I had to turn to look at him with my left eye. I had lost my peripheral vision. We got home within minutes and I remember holding onto the walls of our condominium. I couldn't walk straight. I took some tylenol and about 15 minutes later my eyesight came back followed by a massive headache. We went straight to an eye doctor thinking that they would give us some answers but no. Everything from my eyesight, to the nerves was great. They recommended I go see a neurologist. I had my first ever MRI and remember the words clearly coming from the doctor's mouth. "You have something in your brain……I don't know if it's a tumor or a stroke….. Come back in three months. If we check you again and you don't have anything in the brain that means it was a stroke. If it's still there then that means it's a tumor.

    Then people wonder why I have a bit of an animosity towards doctors here in Laredo. That same day, my mother made all the calls possible and we were able to find a neurologist in San Antonio and drove there the following day. I thought I was going to die. I had only held my son for six months in my arms. My mind was racing with pain, anger, guilt, sadness. As soon as we arrived in San Antonio, the neurologist there performed another MRI scan of the brain and found that there was a blood clot in the brain. The following day they sent me to a cardiologist and I had an echocardiogram done. It was an atrial septal defect.Basically a hole found in between the chambers of my heart. Within two weeks I got a procedure done where they went into my groin through a catheter and placed a small implant for closure.

So now I was the 25 year old who had just gone through a stroke, had a six month old baby and a marriage that was on the brink of divorce.

Around the same time, checkup after checkup, the doctor ordered a complete blood count. Turns out I have a genetic mutation (MTHFR) that affects my body's ability to process amino acids thus contributing to health conditions such as depression, mental health conditions and certain types of cancer.

I was only trying to focus on one thing at a time and doctors had just told me that it was nothing major and to just make sure that I take vitamins to replenish what my body wasn't able to produce. The only thing that I was focusing on was making sure that I take my blood thinners on a daily basis, covering my bruises that I'd get as a result of the medication, taking care of my 7 month baby, and of course myself.

I'm never going to forget my son's first birthday in March. I was wearing a pink and gray dress with long sleeves and leggings underneath to cover up my bruises. I was making sure that I smiled every second and made sure that the pain in my chest was nowhere to be seen. I wasn't happy. I wasn't in love with myself. I only cared about my baby boy and was making sure that he got the best life possible. My husband at the time was and still is a great father to our teenager now. However our relationship was at a pivotal point. There was no love and passion. We let our everyday things get in the way. I wasn't content but managed to stay in the marriage for our little one. My parents had both been divorced before and I didnt want to fall in that same cycle. We stayed together until the following year when I decided to call it quits in 2011.

    Divorce was common in our family . Negative advice was common in that situation. Get the divorce over and done with. Get as much money from him. You're not going to get along with him. I knew that what I didn't want was for my child to not be without a father. I made it a point that even though we weren't a great fit as husband and wife, I was going to make sure that we got along no matter what. Twelve years later we are still going strong. Co-Parenting has had its ups and downs but we have made it work. Our teenager knows that his dad, his stepdad and myself are all on the same page to his upbringing. We love him tremendously and for that reason we will always be civil.

One of the factors that led to my stroke was stress. I let it take over my life, especially my body. I let it manifest over me. It didn't help that I kept these feelings inside. They call stress the "silent killer" for a reason.

I purchased a book on awareness that I re-read over and over and over. It helped me to identify my feelings. I learned to be instinct and in control of what feelings I allowed to enter and leave my body. I remember doing these exercises that would require you to think of moments in your life where you felt happiness, joy, anger, frustration, etc. I was teaching myself how to identify these moments in my life and connect them to these feelings. I'd have to ask myself, "When I feel happy, where in my body am I feeling it? When I feel sad, "Where do I feel it? "When I want to throw someone out the window, where do I feel it? Once I was able to realize where in my body I would feel these moments, I felt a sense of control. Control of my own body. I wasn't going to let anyone or anything have control over what feelings were entering or leaving my body.

During my divorce year I moved into my sister's house for about six months, then to my parents house. I had taken out a small loan to help pay for the enclosing of the garage to turn into a bedroom. I remember telling myself that I would pay it off within two years and make sure that I buy myself a house for my son and I. This was the first time that I remember manifesting that thought and not letting anything get in the way of my decisions or choices.

    Two years later, my best friend (husband now) had also gone through a divorce and we had decided to start dating. We had met in 2001 and stayed friends ever since. We always knew there was a connection but the universe or whatever you wish to call it would get in the way and not allow us to be together until we grew up. And that's exactly what happened. Fourteen years after we met, I was 33 years old, with a beautiful five year old boy, we got married in August of 2015. We had our daughter two years later. I remember the face that my son made when our "gender reveal" party made it known that we were expecting a girl. My son ran and cried in the restroom over that result. You should see how they get along right now. Nine years later and he loves her unconditionally. Always worried about why I give her my coffee, or why she's eating too much candy or why she spends too much time on the phone. The only thing that I tell him is, "Second child baby. You tend to be a bit more calmer and not go to the extent that I did in not letting you taste any carbonated drinks until you were about 7 years old!" He'll see when he's older.

Eight years of marriage and my husband and I are stronger in our relationship. We have had our ups and downs but have managed to talk constructively, think before we speak and most importantly, respect each other. With children to look up to you, it has been important to understand that we are their role models. It can be challenging at times but awareness is the key.

I dedicate this book to my two children that have made me the happiest human being in the world. I will continue to strive in this world just knowing that they exist. Nothing is greater than the love that we give them.

Part One: Let's Do This!

You spend 240.00 a month on a cleaning lady that comes to your house once a week. 99.00 a month at the gym for your one year contract.You spend 60.00 per month on your gardener for your lawn. You signed up for "prep meals" that you pay 100.00 weekly. You are paying for these services on a monthly basis. You take care of your house, your lawn, your body.

What about your mind? How do you feel emotionally throughout the month? Have you ever thought about your feelings? On a monthly basis, how many days do you feel happy? How many days are you stressed? tired? Irritated? Have you given your mind the proper fuel of happiness in order to be stable?

You hire a coach for your child's basketball team. The swim instructor that will teach your children the different types of swim strokes. The soccer coach that will take your child to the championship. What about a coach for your life? Don't you deserve to give your mind the best life possible. Because I can guarantee that if you are fueling your life on a monthly basis with stress, anxiety, overload of work, or feelings of emptiness, your body will start accepting that fuel and you will start feeling that physically now. By that I mean you will start with illnesses, body pains, aches, doctor visits. You deserve to be happy. We have only one life to live and we owe it to ourselves to give ourselves the best life possible.

    I welcome you to the first day of the rest of your life. You have decided that you want to be a better person and you owe it to yourself to live your most fulfilling life. Know that this is a process and I am so glad that you have chosen me to guide you through this journey. You are not alone. I will be here for you every step of the way. We will be working together so that I can guide you, motivate you, and make you believe in yourself at the end of this!
    You have no idea how proud I am of you making this commitment. You have taken your first step to beautify your life. There's nothing like being in control of yourself and of your future. I know that you want to find fulfillment, empowerment, self-confidence in everything that you do. We are going to be getting in touch with our mind and our heart, and be able to

work on those obstacles in your life that are getting in the way.

Today you are here to steer away from negativity. You have decided that you want to be a better version of yourself. You want to fuel your mind with positive thoughts, feelings and emotions. We are going to be looking into different topics throughout this journal. At any time while reading this book, pause, take a deep breath, and know that your life is starting to change because YOU have chosen to.

GRATITUDE

The first step to living a happier life is to become aware of your surroundings. It is with this that you will find more reasons to smile.
Let's take a look at the word *Gratitude*

The state of being grateful

"Gratitude." Merriam-Webster.com Dictionary, Merriam-Webster, https://www.merriam-webster.com/dictionary/gratitude. Accessed 14 May. 2023.

We have so many things to be grateful for. There are many things that we take for granted or don't even consider. We shouldn't be thinking of these things once a year only on Thanksgiving.
Our children, jobs, family, and health are the first things that come to mind. My list can go on and on.

For your first exercise, you will be making a list of things in your life that you feel grateful for. When thinking of these joys in your life make sure that you find a purpose/reason why you feel grateful for these things. We are going to become aware of everything around us and see how wonderful our life is and how it is only going to get better.

EXERCISE #1

Things that I am grateful for are: Reasons:

_____   _____
_____   _____
_____   _____
_____   _____
_____   _____
_____   _____
_____   _____
_____   _____
_____   _____
_____   _____

CONTINUE IF YOU CAN! DON'T WORRY IF YOU CAN'T!

_____   _____
_____   _____
_____   _____
_____   _____

AWARENESS

How do you feel right now?_____
You see, the point of gratitude is not just making your list. It's being able to identify the purpose for each thing we are grateful for. I'm grateful that I have a house that my spouse and I have created. I'm grateful that it's not just a house but our home. My courtyard that I get to enjoy every afternoon, The pantry filled with food. The dogs that greet me as I get home. I'm grateful for the dishes I have to clean because that means that I can provide food for my family.
I'm grateful for the house that needs cleaning because that means that I've given my children a place to come home to.

When this happens, when we are feeling grateful, we start appreciating all these things and guess who isnt in an irritated mood anymore for the dishes, the clothes, taking kids to practice, having to wake up in the morning, putting on makeup and all your day to day things.

Before I'd remember that I'd let these things get to me. I'd feel stressed, frustrated, irritated and anything negative you can imagine. Now you see me saying "thank you dust" as I'm sweeping the floor!

It's all about attitude. We need to realize that the more grateful we are for all these things the less negative impact it will have on our body…on our life. This isn't something that happens overnight. This is a process and you have realized that now you will be in control of your body, feelings, emotions and most importantly your life.

Your job for the next few days is to identify one thing per day that you are grateful for. You cannot list any of the things that you mentioned in exercise one. The point of this next exercise is to become aware of the smallest things in your life all around you.

Example: Today I am grateful for the dogs that greet me for the reason being that they love me unconditionally and are always happy to see me everyday.

Example: Today I am grateful for the little voice that comes out of my daughter's body for the reason being that she will grow older and I won't have that little voice to depend on me.

Realizing these small things will have a strong effect on your well being.

EXERCISE #2 (see you back in a week!)

Day 1: Today I am grateful for _____

for the reason being that _____

_____

_____

_____

_____

_____

_____.

_____

_____

_____.

Day 2: Today I am grateful for _____

for the reason being that _____

_____

_____

_____

_____

_____

_____.

_____

_____

_____.

Day 3: Today I am grateful for _____

for the reason being that _____

_____

_____

_____

_____

_____

_____.

_____

_____

_____.

Day 4: Today I am grateful for _____

for the reason being that _____

_____

_____

_____

_____

_____

_____.

_____

_____

_____.

Day 5: Today I am grateful for _____

for the reason being that _____

_____

_____

_____

_____

_____

_____.

_____

_____

_____.

Day 6: Today I am grateful for _____

for the reason being that _____

_____

_____

_____

_____

_____

_____.

_____

_____

_____.

Day 7: Today I am grateful for _____

for the reason being that _____

_____

_____

_____

_____

_____

_____.

_____

_____

_____.

By now you should've had at least a week since you started reading this book. You have felt a sense of happiness, wholeness in your body. Did you catch yourself noticing everything around you? Are you looking at everything in a different perspective than before? Remember that the word gratitude means "a state of gratefulness." It is amazing to feel so fortunate to have what we have in our life on a daily basis. Every little problem/situation/stressor in our life starts diminishing and we start enjoying life to the fullest.

Practice appreciating everything around you daily and you will notice a difference in the way you respond to negative or stressful situations in your life. We don't let these things affect us the way they did before. You are aware and more grateful now. More grateful for everything you have, not everything you want. You are now living in the present instead of worrying about the future. We all have good and bad days, but it is our responsibility to understand that we should aim to have a majority of good days in our lives. Being grateful makes us more humble to the world. It shows us how much empathy we can have to others.

You have been working hard to become aware of your surroundings. You are looking at life with a new perspective and are appreciative of the things that surround you. You can look at the smallest thing like a plant, a couch, a table and be grateful that you have these things that serve a purpose for yourself and your well being. The dirty dishes are not there to irritate you. They have more meaning than just being dirty. If you didn't have dishes to clean, you'd have nowhere to place your food. You are able to provide for your family. You are grateful for the food that you cook, serve, and feed your family daily. Don't stop appreciating everything around you. You have one life to live and have every right to enjoy every second of it.

Our life will be filled with ups and downs. We have fallen multiple times in our life and have been able to rise above it. The falls are part of life. They will always be there. It is the way we rise that will determine who we become. Our past has shaped us to become who we are. Everything positive and negative in your past has made you YOU. We want to make sure that our past has shaped us to become better human beings. Do we continue with the negative patterns in our life and let them be embedded into our childrens' future? Do we learn from our past and break those cycles?

Remember that gratitude is an important component of happiness. If you have a lot to be grateful for, you'll naturally be happy, too. Make gratitude a habit. Ask yourself what you're grateful for several times each day. Set up trigger points, such as when you take a shower, put on your shoes, start your car, walk into your place of work, take off your shoes, and get into bed. These are just a few ideas. Think about your own life. What are your current morning and evening routines? Use those routines to remind you to be grateful.

DISCOVERY

We first need to dive in and identify our mental well being. How are you feeling on a monthly, weekly or daily basis? Have you ever been aware of your emotions? We need to balance our emotions. We can't live our lives with negative feelings and thoughts all the time. This will lead to stress and anxiety thus leading to illnesses, sickness, lack of motivation and low energy.

We have already been aware of the things in life that we feel grateful for. Now, we need to identify our feelings and emotions so that we can get to the root of it. Being able to recognize your emotions will help you understand where your energy is going.

EXERCISE #3

For this next exercise I want you to identify and circle how satisfied you are with the following:

Relationship (spouse/partner)	very satisfied	somewhat satisfied	not satisfied
Job	very satisfied	somewhat satisfied	not satisfied
Money	very satisfied	somewhat satisfied	not satisfied
Health	very satisfied	somewhat satisfied	not satisfied
Social Life	very satisfied	somewhat satisfied	not satisfied
Eating habits	very satisfied	somewhat satisfied	not satisfied
Children	very satisfied	somewhat satisfied	not satisfied

(Choose 1 out of the 7 above on page 34)
What area in your life would you like to improve?_____.

Why do you feel that you are "somewhat satisfied" or "not satisfied" with this area of your life?

_____

_____

_____

_____

_____

_____

_____

_____

Why would you like to improve this?_____

_____

_____

_____

_____

_____

_____

What would you like to do to improve this area of your life?

(example: If you chose "relationship," you can think of ways to improve. For example: going on date nights, talking more about our feelings, respecting each other, hug and kiss more often)

(example: If you chose "eating habits," you can think of ways to improve. For example: eat more vegetables, eat more fruit, cook more at home, limit sugar intake, drink more water)

1._____

2._____

3._____

4._____

5._____

(Choose a new one out of the 7 on page 34)
What area in your life would you like to improve?_____.

Why do you feel that you are "somewhat satisfied" or "not satisfied" with this area of your life?

_____
_____
_____
_____
_____
_____
_____
_____

Why would you like to improve this?_____

_____
_____
_____
_____
_____
_____

What would you like to do to improve this area of your life?

(example: If you chose "relationship," you can think of ways to improve. For example: going on date nights, talking more about our feelings, respecting each other, hug and kiss more often)

(example: If you chose "eating habits," you can think of ways to improve. For example: eat more vegetables, eat more fruit, cook more at home, limit sugar intake, drink more water)

1._____

2._____

3._____

4._____

5._____

(Choose a new one out of the 7 on page 34)
What area in your life would you like to improve?_____.

Why do you feel that you are "somewhat satisfied" or "not satisfied" with this area of your life?

_____

_____

_____

_____

_____

_____

_____

Why would you like to improve this?_____

_____

_____

_____

_____

_____

_____

What would you like to do to improve this area of your life?

(example: If you chose "relationship," you can think of ways to improve. For example: going on date nights, talking more about our feelings, respecting each other, hug and kiss more often)

(example: If you chose "eating habits," you can think of ways to improve. For example: eat more vegetables, eat more fruit, cook more at home, limit sugar intake, drink more water)

1._____

2._____

3._____

4._____

5._____

Happiness

"Happiness is like a butterfly: the more you chase it,
the more it will elude you,but if you turn your attention
to other things,
it will come and sit softly on your shoulder."
– Thoreau

Even a perfect relationship and perfect job can become old and bitter after the newness wears off. We don't need to live in a perfect location or have the ideal career to be happy. Nothing is perfect all the time. The imperfections are perfect all around us. Look around and see the beauty in everything. Let's aim to make each day count. Studies find that the happiest of people are fairly happy on a regular basis. With this we can learn to fuel our body with positive emotions frequently, leading to happiness surrounding us all the time without even searching for it.
    These exercises that you have been reflecting on have been eye openers for you. You are finding your happiness by discovering how you feel with your relationships, job, eating habits, etc. You are self reflecting on all these factors and narrowing them down to which ones need some adjusting. When we

become aware of how we feel with people and things around us, we open our mind to better our lives.

    Being aware of our feelings is the key foundation to live a life full of happiness. When you feel truly happy and content with your life, any problem can feel like a rock in a river. You can move it away from your path, ignore it and move along, build something with it, or turn it into an opportunity for you to learn. Problems and stressors like rocks will always be on this earth. We need to learn how to manage these things and not let them control us. Like I've said before, we look at these things as opportunities for us to learn and be better human beings for ourselves!

    Let's continue discovering our mental state and dive deeper into our path to happiness. What are you fueling your mind with throughout the week, month? We need to be aware of our feelings weekly and monthly, not yearly. A great analogy that I love to use is think of how often you pump gas. It's definitely not yearly! Let's assume it's at least once a week that you fill your gas tank. By next week, depending on how much you've driven, you will need to refuel again. Our mind should be replenished and refueled on positive feelings and emotions in order to live a healthier and happier life. What is going to happen if

we keep on refueling our life with negative feelings, emotions and people that bring us down?
Our mental state will take a toll in the long run along with your well being and health.

EXERCISE #4

Identify and circle which feelings/emotions you experience on a weekly basis?

Happiness	always	somewhat	never
Joyful	always	somewhat	never
Energetic	always	somewhat	never
Stressed	always	somewhat	never
Tired	always	somewhat	never
Anxious	always	somewhat	never
Sad	always	somewhat	never
Nervous	always	somewhat	never
Anger	always	somewhat	never

********We can work on the following questions through the course of a week so you can address one feeling per week.*

Date: _____

Which feeling/emotion in your life would you like to improve this week?

_____.

Why would you like to address this feeling/emotion?_____

_____
_____
_____
_____
_____
_____
_____
_____
_____
_____
_____
_____
_____.

What is stopping you from following through with this feeling/emotion?_____

_____
_____
_____
_____
_____
_____
_____
_____
_____
_____

What changes in my behavior do I need to make in order to achieve this?_____

_____

_____

_____

_____

_____

_____

_____

_____

Reflection:

Did anything happen this week that made me aware of the feeling that I was working on?

_____
_____
_____
_____
_____
_____
_____
_____.

How did I react?_____.

What did I do to adjust that behavior?_____
_____
_____
_____
_____
_____
_____
_____
_____

Date: _____

Which feeling/emotion in your life would you like to improve this week?

_____.

Why would you like to address this feeling/emotion?_____

_____
_____
_____
_____
_____
_____
_____
_____
_____
_____
_____
_____
_____.

What is stopping you from following through with this feeling/emotion?_____

_____
_____
_____
_____
_____
_____
_____
_____
_____
_____

What changes in my behavior do I need to make in order to achieve this?_____

Reflection:

Did anything happen this week that made me aware of the feeling that I was working on?

_____

_____

_____

_____

_____

How did I react?_____.

What did I do to adjust that behavior?_____

_____

_____

_____

_____

_____

_____

_____.

Date: _____

Which feeling/emotion in your life would you like to improve this week?

_____.

Why would you like to address this feeling/emotion?_____

_____
_____
_____
_____
_____
_____
_____
_____
_____
_____
_____
_____
_____
_____

What is stopping you from following through with this feeling/emotion?_____

_____

_____

_____

_____

_____

_____

_____

_____

_____

_____

_____

What changes in my behavior do I need to make in order to achieve this?_____

_____

_____

_____

_____

_____

_____

_____

_____

_____

_____

Reflection:

Did anything happen this week that made me aware of the feeling that I was working on?

_____

_____

_____

_____

_____

_____.

How did I react?_____.

What did I do to adjust that behavior?_____

_____

_____

_____

_____

_____

_____

_____.

Attention

You have been busy these past few weeks in addressing the feelings/emotions that you experience on a weekly basis. The fact that you are aware of this is a plus. Remember that awareness is the first step of you owning your own life. With these exercises you are recognizing what feelings you are letting in and out of your body. You have more control over these emotions now. We are recognizing what type of "fuel" we are pumping into our mind and body. We are in touch with our feelings and our body. Being aware of your emotions and feelings will make you realize that you have complete sovereignty over your mind.

This next exercise will focus on the attention that you give to things and people around you. This will help you realize where your attention is going on a weekly basis. Is your attention at work the majority of the day? What about when you get home? Do you continue working? What about your spouse? Do you greet each other with affection? Kiss? Hug? Talk during dinner? Is your attention mainly focused on your children (if applicable). Do you give yourself time to get home and relax?

Sometimes our attention is focused on one area throughout the week. For example, you might have a deadline at work and know that you need to put in extra time in order to meet the deadline. You might need to focus on taking your children to practices, events, etc. on specific weeks.

We need to realize that there is nothing wrong with you placing attention in one area throughout the week. The skill that we are acquiring is "awareness and discovery." Are you aware that you haven't paid attention to your husband/wife? Are you not eating correctly because you're too busy with another aspect in your life? We want to make sure that we address the issues before it's too late. What do you think will happen if a year goes by and you don't give attention to your spouse, your health, your children, etc?

EXERCISE #5

Identify about how much attention you give to the following on a weekly basis

Partner/Spouse	80%	60%	40%	20%	n/a
Children	80%	60%	40%	20%	n/a
Work	80%	60%	40%	20%	n/a
House	80%	60%	40%	20%	n/a
Yourself	80%	60%	40%	20%	n/a

Why do you think you put ___% to your _____?

Why do you think you put ___% to your _____?

Why do you think you put ___% to your _____?

Why do you think you put ____% to your _____?

Why do you think you put ____% to your _____?

(reflection)

How can I balance my life and everything around me? Try thinking: What can I start doing differently?

STRESS

A state of worry or mental tension caused by a difficult situation

-world health organization

The mini-stroke that I had in 2009 was based on many factors, stress being one of them. I let stress get in the way of my life. I let it fill my body with negative feelings leading to physical problems. I knew that I didn't want to live my life like this. After my divorce in 2011 I remember that I purchased a book on awareness. I was able to teach myself how to identify my feelings. I learned to be instinct and in control of what feelings I allowed to enter and leave my body. I remember doing these exercises that would require you to think of moments in your life where you felt happiness, joy, sadness, grief, anger, etc. I was teaching myself how to connect these moments in my life to these feelings.

When I felt happy, where did I feel it? When I felt angry, where could I feel it? When I wanted to throw someone out the window, where would I feel it? I felt a sense of control. Control of my own body. The only person that was going to be in control of the feelings entering and leaving my body would be me.

Why do we let other people's problems affect us? Why did I let others have control over me? Are we not strong enough? Questions that I've asked myself over the years that have led me to become who I am. We are the only ones in control of our body and mind.

There are two types of stressors in our life. The ones that we can control or solve and the ones that we have no control over. We will start out with the ones that we can change or solve.

Scenario
We wake up in the morning, get dressed, prepare our coffee and off to work we go. We work, have lunch, continue working, and drive home at the end of the day. We may or may not have the strength to exercise, make dinner, shower and go to bed. Ready to start again? If only it were that simple.

We forgot to add: getting the kids ready for school, preparing lunches, making breakfast, changing wardrobe because coffee spilled on your new shirt, flat tire on the way to work. Call your boss and let them know you're running late. Drop kids off at school, get to work and realize that a deadline has been changed to today instead of tomorrow.

    We program our body to be non-stop throughout the day. We fall into the same routine where we know what to expect. This can make your day feel more at ease because we have an idea what to expect. Hence, when we have unexpected circumstances or situations, or in this case "stressors" in our life, our body starts releasing cortisol (the steroid hormone that helps the body respond to stress). Now, normal levels of cortisol are okay. When we wake up in the morning we release cortisol. These levels can regulate your blood sugar, blood pressures, strengthen your heart muscle and much more things we aren't aware of. This is our body's natural way that has kept us alive.

    If your life is in full gear and high stress all the time, then the release of too much cortisol will have a negative impact on your body. This being the result of weight gain, digestive problems, heart disease, increased blood sugar, etc.

    It is important that we find ways to cope with these stressors in our life. We need to learn how to ask ourselves, "Is this something that can be solved?"

Let's turn a problem into an opportunity. Everything negative that we've been through has made YOU who you are now! And that is something positive! We are going to work together to find ways to fix these "stressors" in our life. We need to work productively with these stressors and change our mindset of what we have done in the past that has not worked for our benefit.

Before we dive deep into these stressors in our life, let's think of these as opportunities for us to learn. We need to remember that life will always be filled with all these different types of stressors on a daily basis.

Exercise 6
What are the stressors in my life that I feel I can change/solve?

1._____

2._____

3._____

4._____

5._____

6._____

7._____

8._____

9._____

10._____

Solutions

Circle 4 from above that you would like to challenge yourself to solve and write them down:

What do you think it will take to try to accomplish this task for #____

_____

_____

_____

_____

_____

_____ Organize your thoughts

_____ Talk constructively

_____ Write things down

  Sleep on it

_____ Eat healthy

  exercise

_____

_____

_____

_____

_____

_____

What do you think it will take to try to accomplish this task for #____

_____

_____

_____ Organize your thoughts

_____ Talk constructively

_____ Write things down

_____ Sleep on it

   Eat healthy

_____ exercise

_____

_____

_____

_____

_____

_____

_____

_____

_____

What do you think it will take to try to accomplish this task for #____

_____

_____

_____

_____

_____ Organize your thoughts

_____ Talk constructively

_____ Write things down

_____ Sleep on it

_____ Eat healthy

_____ exercise

_____

_____

_____

_____

_____

_____

_____

_____

What do you think it will take to try to accomplish this task for #____

_____

_____

_____

_____ Organize your thoughts

_____ Talk constructively

_____ Write things down

_____ Sleep on it

_____ Eat healthy

_____ exercise

_____

_____

_____

_____

_____

_____

_____

_____

We were able to identify the things around our daily life that cause us certain types of feelings. With our previous exercises we have been able to identify how we feel on a daily basis and what causes us to feel that way. By being aware of our feelings we are already ahead of the game. We have more control of our mind and body.

If we can change our mindset and not look at these things like stressors rather than challenges, we can become better versions of ourselves and live a happier life. We can shift our mind and think that these stressors are not happening to us. They are happening for us. For us to learn and move on. For us to be better people. For us to break our old cycles and not continue doing this to our body. We deserve to be at peace with ourselves.

If we can control these stressors in our lives and not let them overtake our well being, we will be able to live our best life possible. Our job when we have a "stressful situation" is to stay thinking positive. Because even in negative situations that we have had in the past, well guess what, we are who we are because of these situations in our life. And isn't that something positive. YOU!

THINK: STRESS=POSITIVE

Now what happens when we stress about something that can't be solved (other people, sicknesses, deaths, family, tough situations)?

I'm not telling you to not feel these things. We have our moments to cry it out, to mourn, to isolate. Remember that time and patience heals everything. We can't control other people but we can be there for them. We can support them. We can cook them meals, help them clean their home, and be a shoulder to cry on. We can listen to them. We can't control world hunger, climate change, or even politics, but we can occupy our time and think of productive ways to help out in our community instead of letting negative feelings infiltrate our well being.

Exercise 7
What are the stressors in my life that I have no control over?

1._____

2._____

3._____

4._____

5._____

What can you do to occupy your time for #____? Or what can you do to help yourself/someone in order to turn this situation into something positive for #____?

_____
_____
_____
_____
_____
_____
_____
_____
_____
_____
_____
_____
_____
_____
_____
_____

What can you do to occupy your time for #____? Or what can you do to help yourself/someone in order to turn this situation into something positive for #____?

_____

_____

_____

_____

_____

_____

_____

_____

_____

_____

_____

_____

_____

_____

_____

_____

_____

What can you do to occupy your time for #____? Or what can you do to help yourself/someone in order to turn this situation into something positive for #____?

_____

_____

_____

_____

_____

_____

_____

_____

_____

_____

_____

_____

_____

_____

_____

_____

What can you do to occupy your time for #____? Or what can you do to help yourself/someone in order to turn this situation into something positive for #_____?

_____

_____

_____

_____

_____

_____

_____

_____

_____

_____

_____

_____

_____

_____

_____

_____

_____

_____

_____

What can you do to occupy your time for #____? Or what can you do to help yourself/someone in order to turn this situation into something positive for #____?

So now look at what we've done. We are being productive and stress free even in these situations that you had no control over.

*** If we have a problem that cannot be solved, then why do we let it stress us out? We are learning to be in control of our emotions and feelings. The key is to stay positive. Look what you can do when you have a stressful situation. You've turned a negative into a positive. You've turned a problem into an opportunity. We can think.... these things are not happening to me…..they are happening for me (You are gaining knowledge as to how to be a better person)… Because in the end, you will still be here, only stronger, wiser…..

You are who you are because of everything that has happened in your past. Example: If it wasn't for your alcoholic father, your parents that died at a young age, your partner that left you for someone else, a traumatic experience or a bad childhood…. YOU WOULDN'T BE YOU!

You are worth more than you know. Our attitude waking up in the morning will determine the rest of your day. What is going to happen if we stop complaining about the little things in life and be more grateful for these things instead? We start **attracting more positive energy** all around us. We start living our best life.

You are an amazing individual and it is time for you to start giving your body and mind the best life possible. It is never too late to change for the good and start appreciating this wonderful thing called LIFE. **YOU own your own Happiness!**

Made in the USA
Columbia, SC
07 May 2024